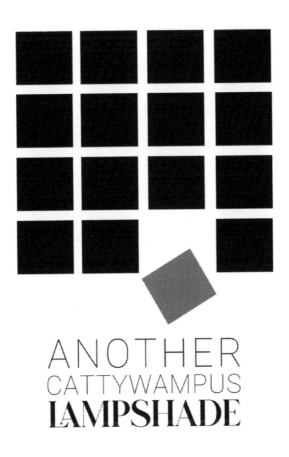

ANOTHER
CATTYWAMPUS
LAMPSHADE

JUSTIN L. JORDAN

Another Cattywampus Lampshade

Copyright © 2024 Justin L. Jordan

ISBN 9798332786037 (Paperback)

Hi. I'm Justin.

I'm not a poet.

I don't know the rules of poetry and I don't want to.

For years, I've desired a creative project that wasn't fueled by my chronic people-pleasing. Not constrained to right or wrong. Good or bad. Just an unshackled expression of what is inside my head with no regard for whether or not it would be "liked" or even appreciated.

One favor I ask (as if buying this stupid book wasn't enough) ...

Slow.
Down.

Chew on these words, as silly as they are[1]. They may have no meaning, or they may have a lot of meaning. The goal isn't to interpret my poems accurately. I can't even do that.

Just sit quietly and let your mind wander for a little while.

---

[1] I mean a poem about corn on the cob? Really? Now would be a good time to lower your expectations.

A Fly on My Toe

I was trying to write about my emotions when the fly landed

on
my
toe

It could have landed anywhere in the world so I yelled at it, and

stomped
my
foot

It tickled my toe, and that irritated me
I am trying to do something calming and peaceful

I need
to process
my emotions

Birds chirp louder, cars without mufflers
Distractions
Life all around me and I want to

shut
it
out

Snuff it out, and tell it to please let me think
Let me write about my emotions, and then

I won't be
angry
anymore

Mining

I went down in the mines looking for self-worth
Realized it couldn't be found in hearts, charts, or even the arts
I excavated gemstones; shiny blues, greens, and rubies too

Realized it couldn't be found in you

I chiseled away rocks, and uncovered ancient artifacts
Dug deeper and found gold that I traded for more tools to go

      deeper

Hard work didn't help and patience is a joke
I tried to flow, tried to lift more weight
But found nothing to take back up

      so, I went deeper

It got cold and dark
Instead of words there were scars
And the scars wrapped around a child like a weighted blanket
And he gave me some licorice and I thanked him

He smiled and said, *"the blanket is heavy and I need to lie down, and you need to go back up."*

And he pushed a button that sent me up in an elevator
And at the top, my treasures were waiting
And at the bottom, my crimson candy

Helicopter

Helicopter circling round and round
What do you see up there?
What is down here that you can't be a part of?

Humming and choppering
You're disturbing the peace!

What happens
when your gas
runs out?

Another noise to drown out
The motors, the machines of this world
Are bringing me down

Is it peaceful up there, Helicopter?
Do you look down from your comfortable seat
and see beauty?
Do you imagine you're the star of the movie
and everyone below are the extras?

What happens
when your gas
runs out?

I hope you're happy up there in your glass bubble
I hope you don't run into any trouble

With your propellers

I hope you find what you're looking for
Before your gas runs out

Mom Water

I came across a rather wobbly lampshade today
It was missing the finial like so many are
I wonder where they all go?
And I wonder how you can afford a $150,000 renovation
and not afford a decent lampshade?

But the rich don't care about the light
The rich are rather blind

You left the price tag on the lampshade, Florence!
It was $89.99 from a local fancy place

Finish your Mom Water, Florence!
Then wash your face

She's probably never even home
She's probably visiting Florida
She probably paid 20k
For a kitchen counter she'll cover with Chick-fil-A

I moved your lamp to the other side of the couch
(where it should have been)

And the shade wobbled the whole way over
Ugly thing too with a dent in it
Ugly couch
Ugly pillows
Ugly art
Ugly, ugly, ugly...

but I like the font on the Mom Water can

Lost and Found

Sometimes things get so messy that

I hide

Sometimes for a long time or years and years
If you have that long
But I don't like messes, so after hiding
Which usually includes running,
Which results in me being short of breath

I seek

I look for beauty in the simple things
Because I can't afford the world's beauty
I look for something to organize because space is free
And getting rid of things makes more space,
But it also leaves fewer hiding places
I put things where I think they should go in this moment in time
(which always seems wrong in the future)
And I feel better about myself, and

I eat

Because I worked hard and I should get more calories for that
But food wrappers annoy me
The plastic packaging, bright colors, ugly fonts
It's all so messy, so

I run

And if I run, I'll probably hide
Which results in me losing myself and
Inevitably something I didn't mean to throw away, so

I pray

The Wall

A tree limb fell and broke my wall
on the ground were pieces of stone intertwined with
branches and twigs of all different sizes
and some limelights were beheaded

I fit the stone pieces back together like I usually do
when damage to the wall is done

>   the cracks leave space for the ivy
>   to grow through

I hate the wall
I know it holds the ground and protects from erosion, and maybe if
the stone was a different color,
but I didn't choose it

I planted limelights and ivy to make it more beautiful
But the trees all around me are dying

They drop their limbs in defiance
And threaten my safety

I hate the trees more than the wall

As I moved some of the bigger branches out of the driveway
An arm of one scratched my neck
It was trying to behead me too!

Maybe the wall needs to be broken
But can I keep my head in the process?

Corn on The Cob

Everyone loves corn on the cob
The kids
The cats
The chickens
What makes it so good?

The butter and salt, I think
The tender crunchy kernels bursting with flavor and butter juice
So much butter juice we sing out in our best Smeagol voice,
"JUICY SWEEEEEEET!"

And everyone laughs and says, "this is the best corn on the cob I've
ever had"

Save some for the cats, and
Save some for the chickens!

But we clean those cobs like wild animals
Forcing kernels through our teeth in between bites
We'll be picking those things out for days
Unless you're one of those people that flosses regularly

Like me

I do it because it's rewarding
And because I don't want my mouth looking like a cob
That an inexperienced corn eater might leave behind
So close to being perfect with random snaggle bits
Begging to be pulled

Or eaten

Walking with You

Four laps at four, and
walking is better than running, and
the tongue requires exercise too, and
the first two are always a challenge, and
my ankles get tight as my jaw loosens, and
by the third we've solved life's problems, and
it kind of feels like a date, and
we find ourselves wanting to go past four, but
there's dinner to be made, and rebel babies, and

now it's raining

So, we run, and
we haven't run in a long time, but
we pretend to breathe like athletes, and
laugh at our silliness, and
I hate the way that I run, but
I can't see myself, and
We kiss because we need a reason to stop, and
because it's what you do when you're caught in the rain
on the fourth lap, and
you wonder why you don't run more

Let's do it again tomorrow, and
we'll see where we end up

Fiber Optics

A man rang my doorbell at 8:08pm
I didn't answer because I could see him on the camera thing
so why would I?

He had shorts, and a ball cap, and one of those jackets from the 90's that
people wore to battle the wind

He looked smarter and more confident than me,
and I suppose it takes confidence to knock on a stranger's door
while the stranger hides away, watching Mr. Confident slowly lose his
confidence because he knows he's being watched on the fancy doorbell
and now he looks stupid

But I'm not the stranger
It's my damn house, and I'm the one being violated
Harassed even!
So, I close the app and march to the door, but I'm too late
He's gone
And now I'm part upset at the disturbance, and part jealous of the
neighbor who gets to see him next

What will they discover that I didn't?
If I had his confidence, I would have asked him how he got it
And once you get it, can you ever lose it?
Or is it yours forever?

Or maybe I'd ask him why he's battling the wind
on the top half?
And if he really does feel stupid when no one answers

He'd probably laugh a superb laugh, and
with a superb voice declare, "I just wanted to know if you were
interested in fiber internet?"

People are so boring
It doesn't matter what they wear

Dysmorphia

I looked in the mirror and saw someone else's hair
It was shocking and jarring and all the things you might expect

I ran my fingers through it and tried to shape it
But it took off running

I sprayed it down with Extra Hold and it laughed,
and I coughed

There were hands around my throat as I squinted to see through the
cloud

Am I silly?
Am I wrong?

Please tell me I'm not imagining it when I see someone else's hair
        and face
        and body
        and voice

But of course, I'm imagining it
Who else would it be, but me?

A Broken Harp

Florence straightened her lampshade today
She pushed on one side too hard and snapped the harp
She went to the used piano store to find a replacement, but the man
there told her all they had were notes

"Quarter and eighth notes and they're five dollars each"

"Five dollars too much!" spat out the frustrated Florence.

"Try the bicycle shop down the street," said another patron

But the bicycle shop didn't have any lamp harps either

I'll rest the lampshade on the broken harp

So, there it sat, crooked and sad
And every so often, someone would try and straighten it
And it would fall off
And they'd say bad words, and scoff at Florence
For not taking care of her things

A Golden Scarf

You can float around in some ethereal state
With your majestic garments blowing and
Waving
Turning
Flowing
Like slow motion smoke
Your hands caressing the air
And completing their course in a circle above your head

Come back to a place full of trees, and whimsical wildflowers
Come back to where there is warmth and things seem more real
Until the chores whisper they're due,
And the dust reminds you that beauty can only be grasped
temporarily

Soon even your garments will wear out

Let the strings tell your story and as they go higher, you go higher
Your feet are lifted off the ground as you whisper, "goodbye"

No, not goodbye
You'll be back
Your feet will touch the dirt again

The smoke clears the room after the flame is extinguished
But something else lingers and if it lingers too long,
It might be grasped

New life sparked!
A golden scarf making its way through the air
And down the grand staircase

Collapsing softly on a cold marble floor

Falling

I found myself surrounded by
such common beauty
Hydrangeas, peonies, roses, and even poppies
Bright, showy blooms that everyone loves

I found myself discontent and disconnected from their beauty
They had become artificial flowers
with no soul

I found myself running to the forest
I longed to be as common as a hydrangea
But the tiresome pull to be something better
caught up with me

I found myself laying down surrounded by
The scent of leaf mold and strange chewing sounds
And the ground opened up

I found myself falling down an old well
And hit the bottom, my fingers bleeding from my attempt to
resist gravity

I found peace as my fingers traced the moss-covered stone
and my eyes settled on the silhouette of a Belladonna bloom
backlit by the bright sky above

Frozen Child

Who is the child frozen in a block of ice?
Does he want to thaw or does he want to hide?

The ice is a wall, and the fire is outside
The heat melts, and the child starts to cry

Comfort him, don't let him cry
and he'll stay chilled
locked in time

Seasons change and his story wants to be told
If he thaws, the fire grows cold

He's a child, he's safe, he needs to be loved

He breaks out of the cave
Full of hate
Full of rage

He breathes fire and ice
He cries glass so that he has something to break
He cuts a path for his escape
And shatters everything that caused him pain

We thought HE needed protection
But WE are no longer safe
What can stop him?
What can quiet his rage?

The father speaks one word
And the boy is back in the cave
A thunderous shout!

And the boy melts away

Party Party
Flank Flank
dibby dibby skeet flat
shook doo
shooky dah
floaty on your do
don't floaty on your mah mah
mah mah
flankity flank
frippity frat tat diggy that?

Not a Birthday Poem

You can still bite your lip on your birthday
Because nothing is sacred in a cursed world

What does that mean, J?

It means that you might find a turtle on its back after an earthquake
After you stain the deck, the carpenter bees will drill holes in it

The best days remind us of the worst
And the worst days remind us of the best

Everything is falling apart as it is being built, and
Maybe Newton has a theory about that

Nine year-olds don't grow beards
That's something to be happy about

Are you okay, J?

Yeah, but I bought donuts this morning for my love, and
she bit her lip

Was it her birthday, J?

Of course!
Why else would I start a poem like this, Stupid?

Carrot Cake

My vision feels dim
I squint but struggle to see
My vision has been darkened and
I try to make out familiar shapes

But everything is blurry and my face feels blurry
I don't recognize anything around me
I hold out my hands
I pray for a gift
I pray for visions, but all I get are nightmares

Where did the solid things go?
I held them and saw them
When the world made sense

Wherever they are
I might be there too

And we'll all get along
And have sandwiches
And sparkling water
And carrot cake, because it's good for the eyes

And we all miss seeing

Hugging Politicians

I knew walking in there'd be crooked lampshades
A halitosis house, designed to impress but full of stench
And pictures of past presidents

I move through the rooms complimenting what I can
Because I'm "agreeable"
Or so my therapist says...

I try hard to make people feel the way I want them to make me feel,
but I can't make people feel anything
Just like I can't bend the stupid lampshade into place

It wasn't made that way
What did you do to it?!

"I'm sorry," cried Florence, "but look at these important people I've hugged"

I don't care who you've hugged Florence!
Help me straighten this lampshade!

But she doesn't try
She gave up trying a long time ago
She just pets her stupid dog and talks about stupid politics

Fitzwilliam

Sweet cat curled up on a faded plastic chair
Mole traps spread out with flags waving in the air
Early light from luminescent bugs
More than last year, more than any year

It's not as hot as I remember
And I think more than I use to
How long could I sit here?

Sweet cat gets up
Stretch your legs sweet cat!
Now he's gone
Five minutes of rest and he's moved to the porch swing

Uncomfortable cat
Should I move too when I'm uncomfortable?
What if the next place is even more uncomfortable?
I long for comfort, but punish myself when I get it

Sweet cat
Don't punish yourself with a bath

The light of the bugs is gone now
and I think I heard a trap snap

Shadow Puppets

Sometimes my heart beats too hard
when I'm talking to a person who has their own scars

Sometimes my hands shake when the emotional weight
of hearing lies forces me into a dark place

Sometimes I want to lash out at the shadow puppets
but my voice shakes like my hands, and
I'm afraid they'll see the fear

I try to understand, but reason eludes me
No control of the broken mirror, and

the shards cut
right through me

Get control young man
Form a plan young man

Give them a poison they can't stand
See their reflection like a vapor, and
ask them why they ran

Never meant any harm brother, but
if I could have poisoned you first,
I wouldn't have had to move on to another

Great Wind

A Great Wind in my sails propels me forward, but I can only move if
you let me
Take away this wind, and I'm immobile
The question of East or West is irrelevant when I'm stagnant

Though I long for progress, I'm halted
Alone and scared but the gentle rolling of the waves tells me
you aren't gone forever

All the beauty and majesty of this impressive vessel means nothing
without the Great Wind to move it forward

I had a plan, a destination, an arrival time that needed to be met
Important people that were waiting on me

It all means nothing without the Great Wind in my sails

I cry out for you to return
Restore my movement!
Get me where I need to be!

But there is no answer
No answer that I like

So, I wait
Floating in the expanse that surrounds me

I wait for the Great Wind to blow through my sails once again
and propel me

Envy

I want to write about envy, but I don't know how

If I was more intelligent, I'd have the right words
If I was more artistic, I'd paint a picture with those words
If I was stronger, I'd use bold letters
If I was more attractive, my words would be in a book
        bound in leather with an irresistible scent
        and a texture that had to be touched

Envy is a green blob that sits in my chest, and suffocates my breath
It's a warm hug that surrounds my heart, but causes my vision to go dark
I want to look at it from ten feet away, so I cast it out
The farther away it gets, the bigger it gets

Its form is a morbid sight
Arms and legs and other body parts stick out of the massive blob
An organism that has consumed other organisms

I see myself next to a pillar of Light and I ask the Light what to do?
I want to get rid of this blob, but there's a hole in my chest left by its absence
The Light expands and engulfs the green blob as waving limbs slowly
evaporate
The blob deflates, and shrinks down into the form of a child

But the child is green
And he's nine
And the Light says I have to nurture him
Which leaves me confused

I don't want to nurture this hellish monster
I want to destroy it

I try to call it back because the void in my chest is uncomfortable, but it
won't return
The Light fades

What does this green child need?
If I had a better father, I'd know how to nurture him
If I was a better man, I wouldn't even know him

Figdy, trigdee, teetle tum
Blibble blabble idy rum
Nokey drokey, squim sqam squm
Figdy, trigdee, teetle tum

A Chariot Ride

Up in the blue and white
        where the view is nice
and whenever I get scared
I go back in the box
      Push 10
           No 12

Higher, higher cause I want to look down
A spark trips a circuit
Now I'm a circus
      a ring of fire ...

Burn, burn because I want to cool down
Do you see me on the ground?

Green with envy, I must go back up
      Push 20
          No 22

Ears popping, life is sloppy
Doors open and close, and the higher I go
The freer I feel, but I can't get high enough
      or free enough

Decorate me, elevate me
Into the blue and white
      where the view is nice
And I swing from the ropes without a net
Because a lion will catch my fall

And I'll breath again

The Graveyard

Maybe this is dark, and you prefer light
I think the two are an odd couple, but a couple nonetheless so don't
break their hearts by separating them

You can sanitize your life all you want
the beautiful ugly will still be there nipping at your ankles

You can busy yourself with self-importance
or even with worthless things
to drown out the noise

I hate loud lawnmowers BTW

But let's get back to the graveyard
A resting place for many important people
Who came up with six feet under?
It doesn't seem deep enough to hide the stench of shallow people
All trying to stay relevant and resisting what is natural

I guess that's why we bring flowers though
Beautiful and fragrant to cover the living stench of fear
Nowadays the flowers are fake, and I find that quite amusing

Precious land manicured by loud lawnmowers and adorned in
artificial beauty to cover rotting flesh and bones

FAKE IN LIFE
FAKE IN DEATH

Should be the inscription on many gravestones

You might want to think about that
when you aren't too busy

Midweek Latte

Wasn't feeling too great the other day
Insecurities and dark clouds choking me
Feeling proud
full of pride
and got knocked down
Went to lunch with a client
My back was turned towards the room, but
I didn't care this time
Wasn't sure if it was a man or woman that took my order
They just seemed sad as they made my latte
Five minutes into it, and I was starting to think this was probably
going to be the best latte I ever had
The artistry!
The patience!

And then it was poured haphazardly into a Styrofoam cup

but the show wasn't over
frothed milk was carefully poured on top, and
I could see the makings of one of those trendy milk designs
being crafted before my very eyes

And then a plastic lid was put on top
and my dreams were crushed

"Here's your latte." Them said. Or said them?
There was a slight smile, although it looked somewhat painful
"Order up!"

My crouton sandwich was ready, and I call it a crouton sandwich
because it's local artisan bread, but the size of a crouton

And I sat with my client and talked about how hard it was being a
"creative"

Mushrooms

I took a walk in the forest to search for buttercups
The little yellow flowers we'd hold under our chins
If your chin turned yellow it was a buttercup
or someone loved you

I found pocket mushrooms instead
Various kinds, shapes and sizes
I stuffed them into my pockets so I could research them later
to make sure they weren't poisonous

But I don't eat mushrooms
I just find them interesting
I think they digest organic matter
Something to do with decay?
I never get to my research, so I can't really tell you

I think next time I'll take a special bag for the mushrooms
I hate the way they feel in my pockets
Some always get smooshed, and they smell like decay

If I had found buttercups
I'd just twirl them and reminisce about the past

If I'd seen a butterfly
I might have asked it where the buttercups went

And I'd also apologize for calling it an ugly worm with wings
and a creepy tongue
when I was younger and afraid
when I decided I didn't like mushrooms

I always throw them back on the forest floor
but when I come back
I always find myself looking for more

Doom Scroll

My rapid eye movements find nothing worth doing
But I can dream and imagine myself

       to be something free

The doom scroll fragments my soul
crushes it into pieces and scatters it across an

       AI generated landscape

Pinch to zoom and I know it's fake, but I love it anyway

I can be him
I can be her
I can be them

I can grow squash, connect the dots
Take a trip and make a list of all the things I'm not

There are pieces of me everywhere, but I'm not whole
I'm in a hole, and you'll never see all the things I can be

When I doom scroll

Another Bite

Overfed and undernourished
I eat a lot
I eat all the things
full, but not
tired of eating
while I plan the next meal

Let's be healthy
Let's eat junk
Let's save money
Let's splurge

The pantry is full, but I'm running to the store
The freezer is stocked, but I'm still wanting more

I eat for pleasure, but it feels like duty
no famine here, but I waste away
you said don't eat from this tree
but meal planning saves money honey
this debt can't be paid

So I take another bite

Mmmmmm
Best thing I ever had
But it will be boring next time
That's the cycle we ride

Until we're out of time

Under the Juniper Tree

Under the juniper tree is where you'll find me

Crying out from the sorrows that have overwhelmed
My throat is tight and full of pain
My voice, a forsaken whisper

Though I long to fight back, I've forgotten how
Raw emotion that once defined me now lost
Hidden in a cold cave, dripping stalactites that echo in darkness
That is what I have become

What caused this? What sin did I commit?
What curse has come upon me?
What toxin is in the air?
Silence, always silence

I spiral down like a wonder machine
And up again
It's over, I'm fine
I'll be just fine

Dizzy and full of cramps I whisper, "enough!"
I don't have a father
I never did and I never will
The juniper tree consoles me

A little food, a little rest
Should I hide the sadness and pretend?
Or should I embrace that this is who I am, and
let the dogs clean up the mess?

Under the juniper tree is where you'll find me

The Ash Heap

I am the ash heap in a cold dark fireplace
The remnants of a light that burned fiercely in the night
Once the source of comfort and radiant warmth
Now the source of filth and a chore that must be dealt with

I once danced, but now I am buried in shadows
Once mesmerized, but now full of sorrows
Like the trees, I was cut down
Fed to a beast with a monstrous appetite

I felt the flames, felt the burn and knew what was coming
But to be useful, to serve a purpose
It felt worth it and I felt worthy
Piece by piece I was reduced to nothing

Was I burned without cause?
It felt like it as I searched for answers that never came
"I'll do the right thing, burn brighter," and other flickers of lofty
dreams
I once danced, but now only in my dreams

My ambitions were poked with a rod of iron
Slowly slipping through the grate as my form changed
A mess, a horrible mess
A couple more turns, and my life was extinguished

But there was hope like glowing embers rising up
I recalled the wisdom of those that gathered around
Those that sang their songs while I danced
There was hope in the cold dark night

And then the gardener came in with a plan
I was shoveled into a shiny pail, and taken into the light
I was mixed with others I never knew, and in bonding became reborn
Carefully spread through a garden to spark new life

Starfish

A starfish lazily makes its way out of a dark rocky crevice
one spiny blue arm emerges from the shadows
and is kissed by a ray of light shining from above
its other four arms are likewise illuminated
as the search for food continues

All around it is life
exotic fish, bright corals
and a deep-sea diver
opportunities in every direction

Two arms slowly go west
three pull to the east
and so, it continues its journey

It makes its way through ocean vegetation
the hair of the sea
dark green tendrils reaching up to the surface
hoping to break the barrier that separates
two worlds

Some friends feast on this abundant resource
but the starfish wants meat
it reaches the edge of a small cliff of coral and leaps

It crashes to the floor
and lands upside down
as a puff of sand disperses all around
a sting felt in arm three from a small fracture
pain for the starfish, but a welcomed little snack
for a wandering crab

Gratification halted
but the wound will heal
the arm will grow back

it flips itself right side up
and it continues onward
Bubbles trail behind as it whispers
secrets in an unknown language
convinced that no one hears or understands
it laughs to itself
it cries to itself

A close friend watches and calls out,
"A fine catch earlier right around these parts.
No doubt you'll be feasting soon, friend!"

Arm four raises to wave as Blue
embarrassingly continues on

And there it sits
like an ancient shipwrecked treasure chest
waiting to be cracked open
a single oyster

Blue's tiny tubular feet move faster
it encases its prey and begins nervously
prying the bivalve's rustic gates open
and there is meat

And something else
a shiny sphere shimmering
in the waving light from above
Blue grabs it with arm two

He leaves the meat and closes the gate
for it had found something far better than food
and the delighted starfish
meanders back to his friend

To give a rare gift
a pearl, a shape without end

Train

Tick tock, the time has come
the train blasts its horn
a deafening trumpet blast
a welcoming siren if you have a ticket

Steam or smoke billows from its chimney
leaving behind a cloud of mystery
choo, choo
the train departs

The haze lingers in the air
I feel invisible but I see more clearly
I look around and see people
that look like me

We smile and nod and make small talk
and then disperse
each going our separate ways
we can still hear the train in the distance

I want to buy a ticket
and go on a journey
but it seems expensive
and I'm busy trying to make money

Tick tock, the time has come
and I feel like I was just here
at the train station
saying goodbye to a friend

Autumn and winter are for the cocoon
And spring is for flight

Untamable

I've soared above the clouds
saw the dawn light the tops of puffy mist, and
wispy windy rivers of fog
destined to rise up

I've explored caves deep in the earth
squeezed through damp crevices
hoping not to be attacked by
eight legged creatures of the dark

I saw a fox run across the field
a wild fox that couldn't be tamed
a lonely hunter in the cold of winter
searching for food, searching for pleasure

A famed intruder with striking eyes
his heart as frozen as the ice he walks on
ready to murder, ready to love

The sun sets on the land
while villages sparkle like obsidian
reflecting the stars
black holes of light and warmth
we're still so small

The dawn breaks again and the light scatters
oranges and reds and fire
light beams shine through the haze
and blood trails in the snow

The fox has finished his mission
he'll sleep like a champion
and when he's seen by someone in the village
his eyes will flicker

And for a second the villager will think they could be friends
he'll put food out, but the fox will be long gone
He heads for warmer weather

World Between Worlds

Where is the maker of this shimmering web?
I want to meet her
I want to ask her why she worked so hard for so little
Endless toil, but she does it so well
Better than all the others

Where does she sit as the little ones gather?
Destruction hits like hail on the rooftops
Tiny blemishes in her stronghold, but she remains unshaken
She'll wait patiently for the big catch

She does it to be beautiful
The murderous artist
She kills for fun
Her prizes don't give her life

Time is measured, and she has one goal
create

Make a gathering place for the weak, and watch them suffer
She's vulnerable wherever she goes
But as she sways in the world between worlds
She shows no fear

She's a master of fear, and she has one goal
create

Murky Waters

Will I drift on murky waters ever again?
Will I hear the sound of happy campers, or irritable
counselors?
I rock back and forth and at times a little too much
The sound of laughter is an addiction, and sometimes I
roll over
and empty my passengers into the brown waters that
carry me

They laugh nervously as they flap their way back to me
I am safe
I am fun

But one day that all changed
I heard screams and gurgles and things got blurry
I remember flashing lights and something was taken

Someone was gone

And the murky waters rose an inch from the tears
And I was pulled from the sea of tears
Punished for something I did wrong

I spend my days on land now, and I get news from the
birds
And spiders that build their homes in me
I've heard rumors about a boy who will live forever
And a woman who will never be the same
And a brother consumed with pain

I wish it never would have happened, and I wish
My creator would put me back in the water
And I wish their Creator would
Stop all the pain

Will I ever be forgiven?

The birds take photos of the blue-eyed woman
And I see light in her eyes
And she still laughs

Nine years is not enough
Twenty won't be either, but she lives

You can travel the world in a boat,
Cross all the seas and be missed
But the spiders often remind me that
The world sometimes takes more than it gives

Fortune Teller

Sometimes, I think I know everything, and
I tell people their thoughts before they even think them, and

I'm right most of the time

My crystal ball unveils secrets through swirling clouds, and protects me
Don't stand behind me where I'm vulnerable to attack

You'll be pushed away

My mind is full of thinking traps, but I'm convinced I have mind-reading
powers, and

I'm right most of the time

Whispers behind me, and the rustling of cheap fabric
Footsteps so loud they shake my brain, and
I want you near, but

I still push you away

Clouds roll in and my future vision dissipates
The one I'm afraid of is inside
The ball cracks and I panic
My security, like the morning fog, ascends into the sky
Now there's clarity as I turn around to face what's behind me, and
realize that

self-preservation has blinded me

Goodbye Florence

So many cars in the driveway
And a dumpster full of stuff
So much stuff
And the grandson drives a little green tractor
that carries a trailer full of
even more stuff

The cars are probably family members
and the grandson's dad takes stuff out of the John Deere wagon
and tosses it into the dumpster

Florence died, and she left a lot of stuff behind
important stuff

The grandson knew it was important because he was yelled at once
for not being careful with it, and
he didn't understand why it was so important, and
his dad roughed him up on account of his sass

Florence didn't have any grandchildren, but she did have a
crooked lampshade

It too was important to her though it caused her a lot of grief
She had come to admire it
Like the enemy soldiers that share their rations with one another
because they know there's a bigger enemy, and
they're just caught in the middle

Now the lamp and its silly hat sit on a heap of Florence's treasures
Trash for those left behind
While the rest get divvied up by the car drivers, and
The neighbors wait for their new neighbors

The Ladder

I climb
I'm a climber
When I'm scared, I climb
When I'm insecure, I climb

When the roof needs to be cleaned, I climb

The view is better up here
Sometimes a bird's eye view is what we need
But my ladder doesn't go that high

When I'm full of pride, I climb
That's the highest I can go, but it's lonely
Little birds fly around my head
But they don't ask me how I am

I try to go back down
But the ladder slips
And the thing that lifted me up
Breaks me

My arm broken and bleeding, and
did you know I wrestle with God sometimes?
He touched my hip
A shattered pelvis
And a broken rib

I was covered in dirt, covered in blood
Ants crawling over my body
And I wanted to get up
> *I need to climb*
> *I need to be ok*

But I'm not ok
I never was
That's why I climbed

Was it all just a dream?

Naked in a hospital bed and covered in my own excrement
I ponder never climbing again
An old woman quietly blots away my filth with a warm rag
I tell her I'm sorry as if I'm apologizing for every wrong I've ever
done
She smiles and starts wiping my dirty feet
And I weep

I weep as if I haven't cried in years
Because I haven't
Because the walls of stone were so tall
Because I climbed too high

I'm just another cattywampus lampshade
another broken exterior trying desperately
to diffuse the light inside